A Grossery
of Limericks

BY ISAAC ASIMOV AND JOHN CIARDI

Limericks: Too Gross
A Grossery of Limericks

A Grossery
of Limericks

* * *

Isaac Asimov
and
John Ciardi

W·W·Norton & Company·New York London

Copyright © 1981 by Isaac Asimov and John Ciardi
Published simultaneously in Canada by George J. McLeod Limited, Toronto.
Printed in the United States of America

All Rights Reserved

First Edition

Library of Congress Cataloging in Publication Data

Asimov, Isaac, 1920–
  A grossery of limericks.

    1. Limericks.   2. American poetry—20th century.
I. Ciardi, John, 1916–   II. Title.
PS593.L54A8   1981   811'.07'08   81–38376
ISBN 0–393–01483–5   AACR2

W. W. Norton & Company, Inc. 500 Fifth Avenue, New York, N.Y. 10110
W. W. Norton & Company Ltd. 37 Great Russell Street, London WC1B 3NU

1 2 3 4 5 6 7 8 9 0

Contents

Foreword I

by Isaac Asimov

*   *   *

How John Ciardi Grew Engrossed

The question I am most frequently asked is: "Asimov, how do you manage to make up your deliciously crafted limericks?"

It's difficult to find an answer that doesn't sound immodest, since "Sheer genius!" happens to be the truth.

It's terrible when you have to choose between the virtues of honesty and of modesty. Generally I choose honesty, which is one way (among many) in which I am different from John Ciardi. Not that I mean to impugn John's character, of course.

I am sure he would choose honesty, too, if he knew what it was.

The last time someone asked him how *he* managed to compose limericks, John said, "What are limericks?"

But then, John is still young (seventy-nine, I think, judging from his appearance) and he may yet learn some of the rudiments of verse, though I understand 3-to-1 odds that he won't learn are being offered and finding no takers.

Another question I am frequently asked is: "How is it you are willing to appear in the same book with John Ciardi?" And to that the only possible answer is "Sheer stupidity!"

Actually, it was not my intention to take part in this *mésalliance,* and I had better tell you the whole story.

I had composed, in leisurely style, and with involuted poetic thought, three hundred limericks and had published them in three books (one hundred limericks apiece, for those of you who are mathematically inclined and are trying to divide three hundred by three—something that consistently gives John trouble).

The first was published under the title of *Lecherous Limericks* by Walker and Company. They were not lecherous, of course, but rather delightful; yet Walker turned down the suggestion of *Delightful Limericks* because he said he wanted the alliteration. (That means two L's, John.)

Whereupon I suggested *Lovely Limericks, Languorous Limericks,* and *Lilting Limericks* as more truly descriptive and as alliterative as well, but the publisher, a ribald sort, countered with *Lascivious Limericks* and we compromised on *Lecherous.*

When the second book appeared, there was considerable head scratching over a title that would capitalize on the enormous cleverness of the first. No less than seventy-eight possible titles were studied and rejected, including, *The Bride of Lecherous Limericks, Lecherous Limericks Fights Back,* and *Lecherous Limericks in the Black Lagoon.*

At the end of a nineteen-hour marathon session on the subject, we had about settled on *Lecherous Limericks Meets Dracula and the Wolf Man and Abbott and Costello,* when a delivery boy who had just delivered sandwiches said, "Why not call it *More Lecherous Limericks?*"

We threw him out, of course, for compound fracture of the imagination and naturally refused to pay for the sandwiches.

But we decided to use his title, and *More Lecherous Limericks* is what it was. When the third book came out, a mood of exhaustion had enveloped us, and when the publisher said sarcastically, "I suppose you want to call this one *Still More Lecherous Limericks?*" I was astonished at the brilliance of the notion and accepted it at once.

The three books, you can well imagine, set the publishing world ablaze. Far and wide, from sea to shining sea, bookstore clerks all over were saying, with one voice, "Sorry, sir, I never heard of them."

I sat back with satisfaction to enjoy my growing fame as a

lyric poet, taking pleasure at my having joined the ranks of the Shakespeares and the Shelleys. (They're poets, John. Dead ones.)

And that's where John Ciardi comes in.

I had met John Ciardi on occasions in the past. That is, I hadn't exactly met him in the sense that it was a voluntary coming together. Generally, I turned rapidly into a doorway as soon as I saw him, but the trouble is that I am not sufficiently visual. I generally ignore the world around me, being deeply engaged in weaving my creative fancies within the labyrinths of my brain. It followed that by the time the large and impressively rotund figure of J. C. had impressed itself on my mind, he was virtually upon me and it was too late to dodge.

Moving into a doorway was worse than useless, for he merely followed me and there isn't room in the same doorway for John and me . . . or for John and anybody . . . or for John.

Let me explain, by the way, that John, at a loss for any other claim to respectability, had decided to be a poet—or at least to describe himself as such to any policeman who approached him for the obvious purpose of arresting him for aggravated vagrancy in the third degree.

Out of weary politeness, everyone has accepted him at this self-evaluation so that he is regularly described as "Mr. John Ciardi, the self-proclaimed poet-or-something."

You can well imagine that John was irritated in the extreme at my cometlike blaze across the firmament of rhyme and decided to do something about it. He sent me a letter which read:

> Since you've shown you can do it, old pal,
> Then I, also, most certainly shall
> Get exceedingly poetical.

This astonished me, for John's prosody is not usually that skillful.

I found out later that he spent considerable time secluded with my books of limericks, counting syllables and sounding out the rhymes till he thought he could manage a passable imitation.

He then proceeded to write 144 limericks in a gross manner only to find that he couldn't get them published unless the name of an established poet accompanied his.

It was at that point that he got one of the few good ideas he has ever had—perhaps even the only one. He challenged me to do 144 also and join him in a coauthored book.

Caught by surprise, but—by the oddest chance—having a free afternoon, I accepted, and the result was *Limericks: Too Gross*, published by the esteemed gentlemen of W. W. Norton.

John was convinced, I am sure, that the book would prove that he was a more delicately skillful poet than I was, so naturally, it turned out to be a great disappointment for him, poor fellow.

He sent me a note which read . . .

> Very well, my old friend, let us see,
> (If you have one more afternoon free)
> Who can win—the best two out of three

in typical Ciardian verse.

The result is the present volume. I expect a snarled invitation to make it the best three out of five any day now.

—Isaac Asimov

Foreword II

by John Ciardi

✻   ✻   ✻

Isaac Asimov: An Appreciation

My respect for Isaac Asimov is a long-standing article of faith: I have been standing for half my life waiting for some reason to arrive in support of my admiration, but it remains, like any article of faith, beyond reason. And well that it is, for I cannot imagine any reason within range of reason to support my quaint regard for him.

Like the earth, the sea, the wind—especially like the wind—the Asimovian presence is an assertion of the primal environment, and the more so as the environment deteriorates. There are times, in fact, when I feel that he is more presence than there is environment for. It will not do to enter his presence until one has placated the first gods. I am empowered by Nil and by Void, by Zilch and by Butkis, and by Framis and Dither, mother and father of Cacophony, to declare that Isaac is the only natural phenomenon capable of rushing in forever to fill his own ever-expanding vacuum.

He has been a horizon line to my life, a constant and necessary point of reference as impressively empty as the far rim of an Oklahoma panorama. Oklahoma once picked up its horizon and blew it away in dust storms. Isaac blows himself away forever. Yet my faith remains that when the storm passes the choking blather will subside and the horizon of some overblown future will once more come into view at the far reaches of the cracked fields.

For there is no evil in the fellow; a talent for inducing nausea, perhaps, but no evil. When, at dank intervals of the soul, I am moved by the Imp of the Perverse to crave pure revulsion, I seek out Isaac's company and he never fails me, for I know that once I have survived the moonscape (dark side) of his wit, I am proof against every desolation of the spirit.

It is not that Isaac's prose is lacking. Nothing in the creation is less lacking. His is a primal blizzard. The utter, blasting overmuchness of it makes nuance impossible and taste irrelevant. Granted such ample qualities in him, what can it matter that he has a tin ear and a sledgehammer touch?

Yet now the fellow, having ridden my coattails to literary splendor by association, has outblown his own bray. He has gone so far as to put words into my mouth. I will not attempt to put any of my words into his: he would not be able to pronounce them. Words, I would have him know, are precious crystals. To put any words of mine into his mouth would be like throwing fine Venetian glass into a wind tunnel, reducing all that might once have trembled in purest tones to crash and splatter.

The art of the limerick (as the truly formal half of this book will make clear) is based on what I will call an ear for chamber music. It is keyed to delicate harmonies and counterpoints, to nuance, and to a seemingly effortless formality and unity.

Isaac has, at best, a fife-and-drum ear. He has learned to boom and to whistle and to strut to the beat, as any robot can. Albert Einstein (a mathematician said by some to rival Isaac Asimov) once remarked that if men were meant only to march they would need no brain, for a merely reflexive spinal cord would suffice for the work. Isaac, in his grasp of such measures, has understood Einstein and has economized accordingly.

These distinctions have been obscured by the sandblast of Asimov's prose. Poetry, however—and even verse—comes contained within a silence and echoes off into the silence that follows. Nothing is more lacking than an Asimovian silence. It is not that the language trembles at his assault upon it, but it does snicker.

Isaac, nevertheless, has a shrewd head up his sleeve, and his performance can be impressive until one stops to think about it. But as Samuel Johnson once remarked of a poodle that danced on his hind legs (I approximate from memory), "To say it is not well done would be a commonplace. The wonder is that it should be attempted."

There remains a point of conscience. I would not willingly defraud any reader. What shall I say to the reader who, having paid for a whole book, finds he has bought only a half book? One might of course razor out Asimov's pages, as neatly as possible, and perhaps recover some of the purchase price by peddling them at a garage sale for illiterates. To razor out Isaac's worthless pages, however, would likely damage the binding that preserves my gemlike offerings. I suggest that the tasteful reader merely skip Isaac's awful oddities and read my perfected forms twice, thus receiving full value, and more —though once the reader comes under the spell of my limericks I find it inconceivable that he could stop at a mere two readings. Yet let me also suggest that the reader's appreciation of my mastery can only be heightened by an occasional glance at the profusions of the robotically admirable Mr.—uh—oh, yes . . . Asimov.

> What Asimov lacks of pure style
> He makes up for—well, once in a while—
>   By the way he can bluster
>   From the depths of lackluster
> To the (almost) transcendently vile.

John Ciardi
Key West, Florida

A New Gross
of Limericks

by Isaac Asimov

*   *   *

1. DON'T STOP NOW

When a certain young lass was still younger,
She requested a fellow to tongue 'er.
    He was two inches deep
    And he then fell asleep;
An event that completely unstrung 'er.

2. HOW IMPOLITE

There was a rude man with a beard
Whose behavior was terribly weird.
    Though he'd screw a long list
    Of girls in the mist
He'd be gone by the time it had cleared.

3. ALL IN THE TECHNIQUE

Said a sweet little damsel, "I blush
At requesting you, sir, not to rush.
    Before pounding the meat
    In a blazing white heat
Why not finger the soft underbrush.

4 . DO YOUR BIT

"My dear," shouted frustrated Wallace,
"Why persist in behavior that's callous?
  Don't just sit there and stare,
  That is mean and unfair
Come and help me unlimpen my phallus!"

5 . SYMMETRY

To moralists, sex is a sin,
Yet Nature suggests we begin.
  She arranged it, no doubt,
  That a fellow juts out
In the place where a damsel juts in.

6 . THAT'S ALL?

There was a young fellow (a cheater)
Who promised a girl he would treat 'er
  To something quite fine,
  Even grand and divine,
And then all he brought forth was his peter.

7 . WHO WOULDN'T?

There was an old fellow named Ed
Who had a bad cold in the head.
  "When all's said and done,"
    He said, "It's no fun.
I'd prefer a young woman instead."

8 . ENVIRONMENTAL EFFECT

When alone, a young woman named Julia
Had qualities rather peculiar.
    And when men were about
    (Short, tall, lean, or stout)
Her conduct was even unrulier.

9 . WELL, HE'S NEAT

Said a certain prim fellow named Hess,
"Though it causes a bit of distress,
    I avoid the last spasm
    Of completed orgasm.
I simply can't stand all that mess."

10. SHE'S GOT GUTS

A shy little thing from Canberra
Decided that sex was an erra.
    It scared her to bits,
    It drove her to fits,
But she did it—in fear and in terra.

11. CONCENTRATION

An ardent young fellow named Dutton
Was simply a sexual glutton.
    He would always make hay
    Nine or ten times a day,
And aside from all that, he did nuttin'.

12. IT ANNOYS THE KING

A courtier, in dazzling array,
Screwed the Queen (Anne Boleyn) one fine day.
    He got little credit.
    He was promptly beheaded,
For the clear crime of *lays majesté*.

13. C R A S H !

On a bridge that went 'cross a ravine
Archibald had been screwing Kathleen.
 The force of his lunge
  Caused the whole thing to plunge.
The worst fucking disaster I've seen.

14. W H Y   W A S T E   T I M E ?

A water boy named Gunga Din
Always wore not much more than his skin.
 Such a costume lacked class,
  But on meeting a lass
He was able, at once, to plunge in.

15. P A R T Y   T I M E

"Here we are," said Attila the Hun,
"Won't you join us in all of the fun?
 We'll slaughter and pillage
  Every last helpless village.
Come quickly, the action's begun."

16. CITIES OF THE PLAIN

A Biblical worthy named Lot
Lived out where the action was hot.
    Those guys out in Sodom?
    Other guys had all rode 'em,
Till God noticed and said, "Thou shalt not."

17. WASTED EFFORT

A deplorable fellow named Sloane
Once called twenty girls on the phone.
    He asked each if they'd screw.
    Each replied, "Nuts to you."
So the poor guy sits home all alone."

18. THAT FINAL TOUCH

Said a cheerful young woman of Graz,
Who made love on the flimsiest cots.
    "With the final hup-hup
    The whole thing just folds up,
And it's fun to end up tied in knots."

19. PREVENTIVE MEDICINE

Said another young woman of Graz
"You ask how much screwing? Why, lots!
    About ten to fourteen
    With perversions between.
Any less and I break out in spots."

20. JUST LINE UP

There once was a wicked old squire
Who burned with libidinous fire.
    After screwing a nun
    And the minister's son,
He took on all the girls in the choir.

21. GOOD FOR NOTHING

Said a fading old lecher named Cardigan,
"I'm afraid that I'll never get hard again.
    What's more, the girls know
    I've this trouble, and so
At the local bordellos, I'm barred again."

22. WRONG!

It was just like old Lester one day
When he joined a young woman in play
    To fail in recalling
    How to go about balling,
So he did the whole thing the wrong way.

23. CONTINOUS CREATION

An astronomess happily sang,
"I've been screwed by the telescope gang,
    They all had a bit o' me,
    For I'm the epitome
Of the grandly impressive Big Bang."

24. IT CAN'T BE SO!

Our delicate verses, limerickal,
So frequently seem anticlerical.
    Each saintly old minister
    Is made to seem sinister
And is filled with a lust quite hysterical.

25. WRONG TIME

There was an old fellow named Morey
And this is his sorrowful story.
    He screwed each of a myriad
    Damsels during her period;
And, gosh, did the bedclothes get gory.

26. SPLASH!!!

Love and sex among mammals aquatic
Is seldom, if ever, quite static.
    When the giant sperm whale
    Impales his female
The results are both loud and dramatic.

27. TO EACH HIS OWN

A New Jerseyite born in Paramus
Offered all of us one of life's dramas.
    He went to the zoo
    And before a long queue
Of men, he screwed one of the llamas.

28. NOBODY'S PERFECT

"The trouble with me," poor old Jack said,
"Is that though my mustache has been wax-ed,
    And I've gook in my hair,
    And I'm devil-may-care,
The fact is that my penis is flaccid."

29. THEY'RE SUPPOSED TO

There was once an unbalanced he-rabbit
Who had the deplorable habit
    Of viewing the cunny
    Of each nice female bunny,
Then using his pee-pee to jab it.

30. ORGY TIME

There was a young fellow named Pete
Who hastened to Plato's Retreat;
    But the girl he would ride
    Had each hole occupied
So he rubbed his poor prick on her feet.

31. LOVELY!

There once was a gorgeous young girl
Who kept the men's heads in a whirl.
>   Her long pubic hair
>   Was resilient and fair
And her nipples were mother-of-pearl.

32. PANT, PANT

There was a tall, gorgeous Valkyrie
Who found her admirers grew leery.
>   When they climb to the spot
>   Where the action is hot,
They cannot dip in; they're too weary.

33. WHY WATCH THE SCREEN?

An exhibiting fellow from Truro,
Underpaid in a government bureau,
>   Earned additional dough
>   With a public sex show
At the movie house, back in the U-row.

34. VA-VA-VA-VOOM

An intelligent lass named Jo Anne
Never lacked an admiring young man
    For her giant IQ
    (Giant other things, too)
Was designed on a generous plan.

35. NO FUN IN THAT

There once was a handsome young pianist
Whose views about girls were the cle-anest.
    He placed one and all
    On a high pedestal,
And the women all thought him the me-anest.

36. STANDING OVATION

There was a young woman named Dawes
Whose costume was made all of gauze.
    When they turned on the light
    Behind her one night,
All the fellows broke into applause.

3 7 . SERVED HIM RIGHT

A young fellow who drove a Mercedes
Was a terrible lech with the ladies.
    What with all his misleading
    He had raptures exceeding,
But he died—and went straight down to Hades.

3 8 . IT'S ALL IN THE MIND

There was a young man so obscene,
He would chuckle at words like "between."
    "Between legs," "between lips,"
    "Between breasts," "between hips."
There wasn't a use he found clean.

3 9 . BOOKKEEPING

A methodical fellow named Wade
Could recall every girl that he'd laid.
    He recorded each poke,
    Every thrust, every stroke,
And precisely how much he'd been paid.

40. WHAT'S MONEY?

A generous damsel named Marge,
When she spied one delightfully large,
    Would kick up her heels
    And, spurning all deals,
Take care of the thing without charge.

41. NONCHALANCE

Once a pretty young woman named Marjorie,
Having dinner within a potagerie,
    Had soup-stained her dress
    And, without much distress,
Took it off, and ate on in her lingerie.

42. PRACTICE

There once was an eager young nurse
Who felt that she had to rehearse
    Every sexual joy,
    Every hot little ploy,
To succeed in becoming perverse.

4 3 . MIND YOUR OWN BUSINESS

There was a young woman named Linda
Who did it in front of the winda.
    The guys passing by
    Would give her the eye
But she didn't allow it to hinda.

4 4 . NOT FAIR

Young Sadie keeps books at bordellos
And she's sore as can be at the fellows.
    All the others turn tricks,
    Get their fill of men's pricks,
But Sadie just gets polite hellos.

4 5 . SUPER-MIDAS

A rollicking fellow named Rex
Was under a fortunate hex.
    It seems he had such
    An unusual touch
It turned everything into sex.

46. IT'S POSSIBLE

A well-brought-up woman named Kay
Would frown, and then haughtily say,
    "If we're speaking of sin
    I will never begin
And yet—well, perhaps—I just may."

47. TRÈS BIEN

There was an old man of Marseilles
Who said to a demoiselle, "Heilles,
    I'll pay you beaucoup
    Give you jewelry, toup,
If only you'll do it my weilles."

48. THERE'S A LINE

With a smile said the lass of Marseilles,
"I admit it's my business to pleille,
    But voilà tout les hommes
    All waiting to commes,
So I cannot oblige you todeilles."

49 . FEARLESS

Central Park was the site of the pass.
"Very well! Here and now!" said the lass.
        Did the fellow then flee
        Pusillanimously?
No! He screwed her right there on the grass.

50 . THE TABLE ROUND

There was once a great knight named Sir Lancelot
Who placed Queen Guinevere in a trance a lot.
        But what bothered the King
        Was: he managed the thing
By serenely removing his pants a lot.

51 . DEPENDS ON THE CONDITIONS

There's a certain young woman named Barb
Who at casual sex is a darb,
        But put her to the test
        And you'll find she's her best
When completely divested of garb.

5 2 . WHOLESALE

There once was a roguish young lass
Who excelled in biology class.
    She thought it was fun
    To curl up with one,
But terrific to do it *en masse*.

5 3 . UNDER COVER

A young lass from the far-off Laurentians
Once made love in a bed of fringed gentians,
    Where the deeds that she did
    Were so much better hid.
They're perversions, you see, no one mentions.

5 4 . FERTILITY RITE

A fine lassie from Auld Edinboro
Was once screwed in a freshly turned furrow.
    To encourage fertility
    With all her ability,
She tried hard as she could to be thorough.

55 . PURITY

A conception that should be immaculate
Will in no way involve an ejaculate.
    But where is the fun
    If that is so done?
For myself, I just don't care to tackle it.

56 . WISE OLD DOC

A kindly old doctor named Grover
Once said, "I am clearly in clover.
    Not being a fool
    I use my own tool
Whenever I'm probing for ova."

57 . VARIETY

There was a young woman named Cora Lee
Who said, "I will do it immorally
    On top and on bottom,
    Any way that I've got 'em,
Vaginally, anally, orally."

5 8 .   A B I L I T Y

In considering active coition
Good girls scorn to impose a condition.
      They let it be known
      They have but to be shown
To adopt any wanted position.

5 9 .   O B L I G I N G

To her boyfriend said pretty Jeanette,
"There are no conditions, my pet.
      You may use any surface,
      Any bump, any orifice,
Whatsoever you want, I am set."

6 0 .   T A S T Y

There was a young woman named Jenny (yum, yum),
Whose charms were delightful and many (yum, yum),
      The sight of her boobs
      And the taste of her pubes
Seemed to herald the coming millennium (yum).

61. IT'S THE SAME IN RUSSIA

There was a young lass of Odessa
Who said to her father confessor,
 "When the fellows surround me
 Pursue me and hound me,
Do you think I give in to them? Yes, sir."

62. DANCING CHEEK TO CHEEK

Ginger Rogers and suave Fred Astaire
Made one hell of a fine dancing pair.
 She had such sex appeal
 But did he cop a feel?
But of course not! The Thirties were square!

63. EXPERIENCE

My boy, don't get married too soon
To do it's the act of a loon.
 It's all right to play
 In the great month of May,
But a wedding takes place in Jejune.

64. WHEW!

To wed four wives at once is Islamic
And yet, on the whole, not so comic.
 To satisfy four
 Is a bone-breaking chore
Unless your sex drive is atomic.

65. VERSATILE

There was a young fellow whose staff
Was, in inches, some twelve and a half.
 It was used as a cue,
 As a baseball bat, too,
(Which always produced a good laugh).

66. TO EACH HIS OWN

There was a young man of La Jolla*
Who kept screwing his wife in the folla.
 Those who passed by would mumble
 Or stub toes and stumble
But the folla was where he'd enjolla.

* pronounced "la hoyuh"

67. THAT TIME OF THE MONTH

Said a woman from old San José
To her lover, embarrassed, "Oh, say,
    This vagina of mine
    You say is like wine—
But today, I'm afraid, it's rosé.

68. DEMOCRACY

Many think it is quite egotistic
To have sex that is just onanistic.
    Most people would choose
    To do it in twos,
Since our system should stay pluralistic.

69. WHAT DO YOU EXPECT?

A Back Bay attorney named Kyle
Kept a very elaborate file
    On the sexual habits
    Of Lowells and Cabots
And found them surprisingly vile.

70. CURRENT PERMISSIVENESS

Through the length and the breadth of this nation
All's now proper on every occasion.
    If a woman feels able,
    Then under the table
Is a suitable place for fellation.

71. NATURAL CONSEQUENCE

A publisher, once (name of Knopf),
Alas, never knew when to stopf.
    He lay down on the hipf
    Of a charming young pipf,
And now he's a charming old popf.

72. BUSY LITTLE FELLOW

An ardent young lecher named Joel
Found himself a most interesting goal:
    To screw all the gals
    Of each of his pals
From the day before New Year to Noel.

7 3 .   O M I T T E D

"Good God, what a terrible flap'll
Be caused by that one bite of apple."
    Said the Lord—but that frolic
    Was sex (quite symbolic)
—That's not shown in the old Sistine Chapel.

7 4 .   O V E R E N T H U S I A S T I C

To his bride said young Galahad, "Kiddo,
Let's screw in each room, beach, and meadow,
    Every day, every night,
    In the dark, in the light."
And they tried it, and now she's a widow.

7 5 .   W O N ' T   F I T

Said a certain young well-endowed Finn,
"I can never do more than begin.
    Though I try very hard,
    My attempt is ill-starred,
I can *not* shove it all the way in."

7 6 .   A M A T E U R   T A L E N T

Mused a certain young woman named Joan,
"I suppose that I'm never alone,
    Since I'm such a good lay
    And I never ask pay
And that somehow the fact's become known."

7 7 .   N O ,   N O ,   N O T   T H A T !

There was an ingenuous Lapp
Who was, it appeared, quite a sapp.
    When a young woman said,
    "Please come to my bed."
He thanked her and took a long napp.

7 8 .   U P H O L D I N G   M Y   H O N O R

Some young women once had the audacity
To impugn my erotic capacity.
    I stilled all their doubts
    With erotical bouts
And thus proved my colossal first-classity.

79. THOSE MEDITERRANEANS

Getting girls for the fellows from Sicily
Involves acts that are winky and whistly.
    But all over Italy
    Fathers then react fitally,
And go after them knify and missily.

80. THAT'S A LONG DISTANCE

A girl from Shanghai had a ball
With the whole Eighth Route Army last fall.
    She was screwed, with a smile,
    Seven times every mile,
The full length of the Chinese Great Wall.

81. OUTSPOKEN

A well-behaved woman named Pam
Once got in a terrible jam.
    When a fellow said, "Who
    Is the nation's best screw?"
She thoughtlessly answered, "I am."

8 2 .   O H ,   H E C K

There once was a Hollywood star
Whose breasts were the largest by far.
  No use copping a feel,
  For her bra is chrome-steel,
A habit men think quite bizarre.

8 3 .   L O O K I N G   G O O D

A bright fellow once met a young whore
Who wore nothing behind or before.
  He looked at her well,
  Said, "Whatever you sell,
I must say that I like the décor.'

8 4 .   F A K E

Do you know why Joe seems to be furious?
He'd been treated in manner injurious.
  He was set for a lark
  With a girl in the dark,
And then found that her breastworks were spurious.

8 5 . SPELLING

Deer hunting is greatest by far.
It's the one outdoor sport I don't bar.
> But that isn't puzzling.
> I like all that nuzzling,
Since I spell the word D-E-A-R.

86 . UNSATISFACTORY

There was a young maid of Altoona,
Who said to an ardent young spooner,
> "It is simply no use,
> Put me down, turn me loose.
Though I come pretty soon, you come sooner."

8 7 . WIGGLE THOSE FINGERS

There was a young fellow from Butte
Who married a girl who was mutte.
> "When she wants sex," he said,
> "And points to the bed,
The signs that she makes are so cutte."

88. NOT SO SMART

In a lane, a young fellow named Cooper
Committed a terrible blooper.
  He had his girl bare
  In his car, unaware
Of a vigilant nearby state trooper.

89. INGENUITY

A woman from old Monterey
Decided to try a new way.
  She got into bed
  And stood on her head
And found the men eager to pay.

90. BETTER THAN COMIC SONGS

An ebullient fellow named Marty,
A raucous lad, rather a smarty,
  Had screwed pretty Mabel
  Right there on the table,
And greatly enlivened the party.

9 1 . H O W ' S T H A T !

An experienced lecher, Stefan,
Keeps a woman upon a divan.
>   Two more on a chair,
>   All three of them bare
And keeps proving to them he's a man.

9 2 . N O N C H A L A N T

A carefree young woman named Nola
At one time in a summer pergola
>   Took care of three men
>   Again and again
And did it on just Coca-Cola.

9 3 . A Q U E S T I O N O F M O N E Y

A little adultery spices
Our lives, but just look at those prices!
>   If they charge all that dough,
>   Men can't buy it, you know,
And there'll be a frustrational crisis.

94. ENDURANCE

A soldier came back with the knack
Of enduring six hours in the sack.
    And without once withdrawing
    He'd keep up with his sawing—
So the ladies chipped in for a plaque.

95. A GOOD SPORT

Make a pass, if you will, at Miss Rogers.
You'll find she's not one of those dodgers.
    At the rooms that she rents
    All the joys are immense
As she sleeps with each one of the lodgers

96. ALL THE NEWS THAT'S FIT TO PRINT

The *Times* tells the world what is doing;
Who's winning, who's losing, who's suing,
    Who's striking, who's stealing,
    Who's dying, who's healing,
But won't say a word on who's screwing.

9 7 . IT'S THE FAULT OF THE ROMANS

An astronomer said, "What's the use!
Our classical knowledge is loose.
    There can be nothing stupider
    Than to name that world Jupiter,
When we all know it should be called Zeus."

9 8 . WHAT A HIDING PLACE!

There once was a genial old soul
Well known for the bank funds he stole.
    Although under suspicion,
    He defied extradition
From the depths of his mini-black hole.

9 9 . PERFECT

The girl who is really unbeatable
Is the one with whom sex is repeatable;
    Who's eternally screwable
    And always renewable,
And who, most of all, is found eatable.

100. GOOD ADVICE

Said a genial, self-confident chap,
To the pretty young thing on his lap,
    "Of course you can't leave.
    You're here to conceive,
And you'll love it, so don't be a sap."

101. SCIENTIFIC ATTITUDE

There's a luscious young damsel, Celeste,
Who, everyone claims, is the best.
    But such secondhand views
    Only serve to confuse.
I prefer a more personal test.

102. LOVING ONE'S WORK

When the men were all absent, Jane drooped,
And she liked it the best when they grouped.
    She worked them with vigor,
    Reducing their rigor,
And when done, felt delightfully pooped.

1 0 3 . SCRAPING THE BOTTOM OF THE BARREL

There was a young woman named Janey,
And no one alive is less brainy.
    In her search for a man
    She has gone to Iran
To wed Ayatollah Khomeini.

1 0 4 . A MATTER OF OPINION

There was a young woman named Chris,
Who said, when she squatted to piss,
    "Men aren't so bright,
    They do it upright,
When it's simpler to do it like this."

1 0 5 . MITIGATING CIRCUMSTANCES

A convinced Philistine named Delury
Had once slain a young poet in fury.
    The corpse, a wine-bibber,
    Had dealt in *vers libre*,
So Delury was thanked by the jury.

106. DESSERT

There was a young woman named Rhoda
As sweet as a chocolate soda.
    It was such a delight
    To screw her at night
Then once more at dawn as a coda.

107. TEMPTRESS OF THE NILE

Cleopatra's a cute little minx
With a sex life that's loaded with kinks.
    Marcus A. she would steer amid
    The palms and Great Pyramid
And they'd screw on the head of the sphinx.

108. WE ALL GET OLD

There was an old lady of Brewster
Who would mutter, whenever I gewster,
    "You're losing the knack,
    Or you're missing the crack,
'Cause it don't feel as good as it yewster."

109. SHE'S NO DOPE

Upon high Olympus, great Zeus
Muttered angrily, "Oh, what the deuce!
    It takes spiced ambrosia
    To get the nymphs cosier
And Hera supplies grapefruit juice."

110. GOOD THINKING

There was a young lass of New York
Who loved fondling her boyfriend's big dork.
    She would stroke and embrace it,
    Then carefully place it
In the spot where her two thighs did fork.

111. OH, DADDY!

A pious young minister's pappy
Had a sex life, diverse, hot, and snappy.
    It shocked his dear son
    When he had all that fun,
But it made girl parishioners happy.

1 1 2 . R E A R   V I E W

When a hardened old rake felt the twinge,
He'd go barreling off on a binge.
    His bawdy-house feats
    Involving girls' seats
Made the hardiest filles-de-joie cringe.

1 1 3 . A P P A U L I N G

Said a lighthearted girl from Salerno
"It is better to screw than to burn, oh."
    St. Paul soon took note
    Of this flagrant misquote,
And consigned her to Dante's Inferno.

1 1 4 . D E C E N C Y   A B O V E   A L L

Julius Caesar would screw a fine quorum
Of girls in the old Roman forum.
    He made watchers pay,
    Or else turn away.
Thus conducting the show with decorum.

1 1 5 . I WON'T EVEN THINK ABOUT IT

A sweaty young yeti named Betty
Had a love in the park, Serengeti.
 An ungainly old gnu
 Who was faithful and true,
With love ready and heady and steady.

1 1 6 . UP IN THE AIR SO HIGH

A well-endowed lover named Walter
In charging his girl, did not falter,
 But he tripped on a stone
 And instantly shone
As a great (accidental) pole vaulter.

1 1 7 . STRAIGHT AS A DIE

A grave Church of England D. D.
Ran off with a nice chimpanzee.
 But do not feel remorse,
 She was female, of course.
The vicar's not queer, don't you see.

118. WHAT ABOUT THAT IN BETWEEN

There was an old fellow named Murray,
Whose wife said, "My God, how I worry.
When we're both in bed,
He's either quite dead,
Or he's finished in much too much hurry."

119. SELF-CONFIDENCE

A young wheeler-dealer named Timothy,
Said, "Why, all that I need is proximity.
Just show me my prey and
Then give me one day and
They'll be screwed with complete equanimity

120. WHILE THE CAT'S AWAY

A doughty old knight of Belgrade
Cantered southward to join the Crusade.
His lady, recalling
That squires knew their balling,
Faced a husbandless life undismayed.

1 2 1 . W E A K   S P O T

The Homeric young fighter Achilles
Was great with the fair Trojan fillies,
    But Paris said, "We'll
    Just aim at his heel."
Now Achilles is pushing up lilies.

1 2 2 . D O N ' T   T A K E   M Y   W O R D   F O R   I T

When they gave me a scroll as "the best,"
They just wrote those two words, but the rest
    You can call out en masse
    (Unless you're a lass
Who'd like putting the thing to the test).

1 2 3 . O O H ,   L A ,   L A

Parisian girls mutter "Peut-être"
Once they've earned their well-known scarlet lettre,
    So when told "Je t'adore"
    They answer, "Encore?
Well—provided monsieur does it bettre."

124. AND IT'S SACRED, TOO

A Brahman who lives in Bombay
Shrieked with horror and fainted today,
    When he found that somehow
    He had buggered a cow.
(Her pleased "moo" was what gave it away.)

125. COMPLICATIONS MAY SET IN

Sex need *not* be at all conversational.
Without talking, it's still inspirational.
    But mind you're not burned
    For many have learned
The act can be baby-creational.

126. ANY PORT IN A STORM

A wily old shiek of Arabia
Said, "My eunuchs tell me that there may be a
    Great dearth of Circassians
    To surfeit my passions.
But my camel's here—labia are labia."

1 2 7 . ALWAYS THE GENTLEMAN

I met a young lass named Roberta
And I did all I could to divert 'er.
        But talk wouldn't do.
        She wanted to screw.
I gave in. After all, could I hurt 'er?

1 2 8 . CONNOISSEUR

When expecting erotic delight,
Make sure that the wine is just right.
        You should always have red
        With brunettes in your bed,
But with blondes, just be certain it's white.

1 2 9 . WHAT MORE IS THERE?

There was a young woman named Ina
Who said, "There is nothing that's finer
        Then my good husband, Howie,
        Who's a real knockout zowie,
Whenever he's near my vagina."

1 3 0 . ENGLISH LOVE AT FIVE

"It is nice when a young lady *has* tea."
Said Jane, "though it may be just fast tea.
    These revels and spasms
    Of tealess orgasms
End up, I'm afraid, being nasty."

1 3 1 . EXPERIENCE LOVE AT ANY TIME

A gentleman shouldn't bring haste for it.
He must see that the lady is paced for it.
    He must kindle the fire,
    Raise it carefully higher,
Producing a connoisseur's taste for it.

1 3 2 . RANDOM POSITIONS

Said John, "In my recent attacking,
Variety seems to be lacking.
    Let's drop on the bed
    From the lamps overhead
And however we land, let's get cracking."

133. MOTHER GOOSE REVISITED

They say Jack and his best girlfriend, Jill,
One nice day went and climbed up a hill.
    Was it water they're after?
    Then why all that laughter?
And how come Jill made sure of her pill?

134. —AND REVISITED

Where is Little Boy Blue this fine morn?
In the haystack as sure as you're born.
    But he isn't asleep;
    He's with Little Bo-Peep;
And just look where he's putting his horn.

135. —AND REVISITED

"As for screwing," said Little Miss Muffet,
"I proclaim here and how that I love it.
    I defy the authority
    of The Moral Majority.
They can take all their preaching and stuff it."

1 3 6 . — A N D   R E V I S I T E D

Jack Horner, they say, probed a pie
With his thumb, for a plum, but "Oh, my
    How the years will produce
    A much better-placed use
For his thumb," the young maidens all cry.

1 3 7 . — A N D   R E V I S I T E D

We treat Mary (of unknown locality)
And her lamb without proper formality.
    Let me ask: Do we view
    A young ram or a ewe?
Just pure love? Or a budding bestiality?

1 3 8 . M A R I T A L   A R G U M E N T ,   P A R T   O N E

It is sad when two loved ones fall out
Over things they should not fight about.
    They should stay sentimen-i-tal
    About all that is gen-i-tal
And make inches no object of doubt.

139. MARITAL ARGUMENT, PART TWO

Said the husband, with smiling urbanity,
"I possess penile superhumanity."
    Said his wife, "But the score
    Of his inches is four.
The rest of it's just his insanity."

140. MARITAL ARGUMENT, PART THREE

Hubby's fury then reached incandescence.
And he said, "My respect for her lessens,
    Because four is the *least*."
    "Not so, you vile beast;
That's its length in a state of tumescence."

141. MARITAL ARGUMENT, PART FOUR

"Four inches where *you* are concerned,
You old bag," said her man, really burned.
    "All your girls," she said, "gave it
    (In this signed affidavit)
As four!" and the court stands adjourned.

1 4 2 . DOWN WITH RACISM

An American fellow from Tucson
And a lady Korean from Pusan
　　Made it sexually
　　(Internationally)
And for that they deserve no abuse, son.

1 4 3 . CRIME AND PUNISHMENT

Please don't tell me that sex doesn't matter.
It will sometimes make ladies grow fatter.
　　And then, don't you see,
　　What was two becomes three,
With that nerve-racking sound—pitter, patter.

1 4 4 . HOPE ABANDONED

Said Mrs. Smith sadly, "J'accuse
Mr. Smith of what does not amuse.
　　He will start things all right
　　Any time of the night,
But then almost at once blows his fuse."

An
Engrossment
of Limericks

by John Ciardi

* * *

1 .

There once was a girl who intended
To keep herself morally splendid
    And ascend unto Glory,
    Which is not a bad story,
Except that that's not how it ended.

2 .

There once was a lady who thought
Only one thing, but thought it a lot.
    She thought yes and no,
    Till at eighty or so
She decided she rather thought not.

3 ·

Said a specialty hooker named Jean,
Who made the Jacuzzi her scene,
  "A rub-a-dub-dub,
  Three men in a tub
Not only come close—they come clean."

4 ·

A rather shy call girl named Sue
Cut slits in the covers she drew
  Up over her head
  When she got into bed—
Three marked "Service" and one "Peek-a-boo!"

5 ·

There were two consenting adults
Who agreed that they would not repulse
  One another's advances
  But just take their chances
And accept the result—or results.

6 .

At chit-chat last week with the duchess,
She remarked, "My dear boy, in as much as
    His Grace is away,
    And it's raining today,
What say we cut up a few touches?"

7 .

An aged Rumanian whore
Taught her daughters the art and the lore
    Of keeping the house
    When shedding a spouse.
It beats peddling ass door to door.

8 .

"I had rather believed," said the earl,
"Room service would send up a girl.
    But we have gone this far.
    And, well, there you are.
And I say, let's give it a whirl."

9 .

There was a promoter named Hugh,
Who promoted a dance called The Screw.
    Disco by disco
    From New York to Frisco
He made it the in-thing to do.

1 0 .

There once was a fellow so vile
All our maids lost their heads for a while.
    Somehow what he lacked
    In breeding and tact
He made up for by sheer lack of style.

1 1 .

"It's your daughter," said Constable Fred.
"She's too flouncy by half. It's been said
    Every bitch has her day,
    But I'd rather not say
What that girl's taken into her head."

1 2 .

There once was a farmer named Hicks,
Who used ewes for unusual tricks
    And went on at such length
    That he'd sapped all his strength
By the time he had turned ninety-six.

1 3 .

One semester a young prof named Innis
Taught two hundred coeds what sin is.
    Not, bad, I acknowledge,
    For a small country college,
But not worth recording in Guinness.

1 4 .

A pious young priest from South Bend
Prayed through long sleepless nights with a friend
    Till she started to swell.
    Then they saw all too well
Prayer can't change how it goes in the end.

1 5 .

Said an overfastidious gent
To a whore, "If you mean to give vent
    To my passions, I hope
    You've made good use of soap,
And have grown to the age of consent."

1 6 .

There was a young lodger named Byrd,
Who woke in the night. Had he heard
    Something stir? Was a hand
    Softly fondling his gland?
Yes, he had, and it was.—'Pon my word!

1 7 .

A Pavlovian student named Zell
Trained girls to respond to a bell
    By shedding their clothes
    And assuming the pose.
He claims that it works rather well.

1 8 .

An ugly young fellow named Weems
Discovered a girl in his dreams.
    At very first sight
    She took such a fright
She woke him with blood-curdling screams.

1 9 .

I can't tell you much about Slade.
He just came for a weekend and stayed,
    Making rather too free
    With my household and me,
And begetting four sons by our maid.

2 0 .

There was a young man named Mahoney
Who was thought of, by some, as a phony.
    He did talk up a storm.
    But come time to perform
He sure had a lot of baloney.

2 1 .

A businesslike lady once baited
The door of her flat with X-rated
  Interior views,
   And, in neon, FREE BOOZE.
Then stretched out on a bearskin and waited.

2 2 .

An angry young fellow once wrote
His ex-girlfriend a rather firm note
  In such lurid detail
  It caught fire in the mail.
—Which leaves me unable to quote.

2 3 .

There once was a Jerry named Ford
Who suggested he might climb aboard
  The campaign express
  If asked, but I guess
The suggestion was largely ignored.

2 4 .

Jimmy Carter came on with a grin
All over his puss. To begin
    It seemed rather cute.
    But it's no substitute
For knowing what century you're in.

2 5 .

There once was a slicker named Dick,
Who, no matter how dirty the trick,
    Invoked the authority
    Of the silent majority
Till he found he could not make it stick.

2 6 .

There once was a widow named Jackie,
Whose wardrobe was getting plain tacky.
    So she married Ari
    And went to Paree
And near bought the town out, by cracky.

27.

There once was an old pro named Spiro,
Who ran out on the field like a hero.
    And he sure was a slickjack
    At running a kickback,
But he fumbled, and now he's a zero.

28.

A word spout named Howard Cosell
Set his sights on the language Nobel
    By overinflating
    His confabulating,
But to blow hard is not to blow well.

29.

There once was a baker of parts
Who wasted no time on false starts.
    He turned out pies and cakes
    And fine bread in two shakes,
Leaving plenty of time for the tarts.

3 0 .

There was an old hornman who jammed
All night with two broads. When they scrammed
    An hour after dawn,
    He looked at his horn
And said, grinning, "Well, I'll be goddamned!"

3 1 .

There was a young lady from Queens,
Who while still in the blush of her teens
    Developed a range
    Of behavior so strange
It stirred rumors of recessive genes.

3 2 .

There was a young fellow who knew
Drinking, dicing, and whoring won't do.
    Which one might suppose
    Is plain fact, though, God knows,
Such knowledge is given to few.

3 3 ·

One evening a matron named Potter
Was debauched by a young squire who caught her
    In the depths of her garden.
    Having done, he begged pardon,
Saying, "Oops! I meant that for your daughter!"

3 4 ·

There was a young beauty named Mia,
Who never quite got the idea,
    Or who wasn't inclined
    To what boys have in mind.
Either way they stopped coming to see a.

3 5 ·

An eager young actress named Hartz
Let directors make free with her parts.
    What else can you do
    When you're just twenty-two
And not yet a name in the arts?

36.

There was a young longhorn named Lew,
Whose card read, "Have doodle. Will do."
    But the best he could doodle
    Looked like a wet noodle
In a shoot-out with my sister Sue.

37.

There was a young lady so nice
She wore rubber pants filled with ice
    Which kept her so cool
    She got halfway through school
With no need of sexual advice.

38.

There was a young lady named Mame,
Whose parents believed it a shame
    To reject all the beaus
    Who came round to propose.
But she didn't. That's not why they came.

3 9 ·

Said Tiresias to Oedipus Rex,
"I'm too old to care about sex,
But I'm telling you, brother,
That queen's a mean mother
And she's setting you up for a hex."

4 0 ·

There was a pragmatic young SPAR
Who would not let the boys go too far.
An orgasm or two,
She believed, ought to do,
After which she'd say, "Well, there you are."

4 1 ·

There once was a cad from New Paltz
Who, among his less odious faults,
Scorned romance as "red tape."
He preferred simple rape
Without what he called "all that schmaltz."

42.

Said an underworked harlot from Kew
After lying all night between two
    Post-Edwardian beaus,
    "At Madame Tussaud's
Ah've seen sports what was livelier than you!"

43.

There's not much to be said for the style
Of the various lairds of Argyle.
    They just flip up the kilt
    And plunge to the hilt
In the lasses they choose to defile.

44.

In Shanghai a lady named Jinx
Got blind drunk on oddly mixed drinks.
    She awoke in a bunk
    In the hold of a junk
With no light but what passed through two Chinks.

4 5 ·

My professor of sex claimed he knew
A hundred and one things to do.
    My girlfriend ain't much
    At book-learning, as such,
But she knows a hundred and two.

4 6 .

There was a teenager named Clem,
Who referred to all girls as "Oh—them."
    Then one night his dad
    Stopped to say "Good night, lad,"
And withdrew with, "Oh, well now—ahem!"

4 7 ·

A sweetly developed young creature
Developed a crush on her teacher
    Who developed a lump
    That developed a bump
That is now her most prominent feature.

48.

There's no help for poor Freddy O'Day.
He felt dismal about being gay.
    Then a willing young bitch
    Tried to teach him to switch,
But he found it just ghastly that way.

49.

There was a young lady named Hammer
With a s-s-s-s—stammer.
    I had gone all the way
    Before she could say
She was dosed. Now I've got it, goddamn 'er!

50.

There was an old farmer named Swift,
Who went into town and got spiffed.
    He woke in a sty
    With a sow standing by
And said, "Now, dear, no use getting miffed!"

5 1 ·

Said Miss Atkins, "Young man, you're a bore!
I don't mind your smashing my door
    And just forging ahead
    Without a word said,
But why always here on the floor?"

5 2 ·

To St. Peter an ex-dean of Goucher
Declared she had let no man touch her.
    After careful review
    He let her pass through,
But he shrugged as he OK'd her voucher.

5 3 ·

A gifted old man from Darjeeling
Read sweet Susie's tea leaves, revealing
    The quite sordid facts
    Of various acts
The pious young fraud was concealing.

5 4 ·

There was an old hooker named Ryan,
Who kept tryan and tryan and tryan.
    She tried all the way
    From Maine to L.A.,
But not even the Okies were byan.

5 5 ·

On a survey of first dates Prof. Ness
Asked girls, "Would you care to undress?"
    He found 8-4-point-6
    Said, indignantly, "Nix!"
But that 1-5-point-4 answered "Yes!"

5 6 .

A pert little lady named Bobbie
Used to stroll through the Fontainebleu lobby
    Attracting the stares
    Of chance millionaires
Not entirely, I think, as a hobby.

5 7 ·

There was a young tourist in Turin
For winin' and dinin' and whorin'.
    But the girls wouldn't do,
    The pasta was glue,
And the wine tasted vaguely of urine.

5 8 ·

Said a porno queen, "Yes, I take care
To give everyone reason to stare.
    But the play of my parts
    Is all for the arts,
Or I just couldn't bear what I bare."

5 9 ·

There was a young lady of Florence
Who could not abide D. H. Lawrence.
    When invited by Frieda
    To follow the leader
She expressed what is best called abhorrence.

60.

We don't know much of Phallos, the Greek.
He engaged seven sluts for a week.
    But the two who survived,
    Upon being revived,
Were too flabbergasted to speak.

61.

The once-esteemed Lady Hortense
Contracted from one of our gents
    A social bequest
    She passed on to the rest
With what we feel was malice prepense.

62.

There once was a girl who drank gin.
That isn't too bad to begin,
    But reiteration
    Shows a high correlation
With behavioral lapses called sin.

6 3 .

There was a young lady named Hope,
Whose Ma washed her mouth out with soap
    When she found her asprawl
    With three boys in the hall
And doing her utmost to cope.

6 4 .

There once was a starving old poet
Who never could sell what he wroet.
    He practiced austerity
    For the sake of posterity,
But he left it not even one quoet.

6 5 .

An Annapolis madam named Gideon
Used to say on inviting a middy in,
    "Now, lad, don't be nervous.
    It gets hard in the service,
But my girls all have soft tums to tiddy in."

66.

A young do-it-yourselfer once screwed
Two pieces together. If you'd
    Like to know what he made,
    You must ask Adelaide
And her little kid sister, Gertrude.

67.

At our last dance a young man named Schacht
Was admired by the girls for his tact.
    When he wanted a lay
    He would bow low and say,
"May I have your next sexual act?"

68.

A young physicist working for Myles
Left a couple of lead-covered vials
    On the seat of his chair.
    When he got up from there
He had an-atomic-al piles.

6 9 .

I've a theory I'd like to propound.
It was not, as some scholars have found,
    The apple aglow
    On the tree that brought woe
To the world, but that pair on the ground.

7 0 .

The old woman who lived in a shoe,
When she had nothing better to do,
    Would bed down her dears
    After boxing their ears,
And relax with a cobbler or two.

7 1 .

There once was a farmer named Jives,
Who grew tired of his seven old wives.
    He gave each as her pittance
    Some cats and some kittens
And herded them out of St. Ives.

7 2 .

To his bride whispered J. Osgood Neely,
"My dear, let us love so ideally
    That nothing so crude
    As sex need intrude
On our Eden." Said she, "You mean—really?"

7 3 .

The groom woke up late the third day
To discover his bride's best friend, Mae,
    Had come for a visit,
    And crying, "Where is it?"
Was tearing the bedclothes away.

7 4 .

There was a young fellow on Bimini
Who chartered a yacht for three women he
    Intended to trick.
    But the swells made him sick.
An ambitious young cad, but no seaman he.

7 5 ·

An ambitious young fellow named Knight
Ended up on Skid Row. He got tight,
    And rolled in foul ditches
    With badly poxed bitches.
And now he has no end in sight.

7 6 .

There once was a young farmer's daughter
Who learned a bit late that she oughter
    Have studied what teacher,
    Her mom, and the preacher
Believed they had already taught her.

7 7 ·

Life is merry in old Monterey.
When the duke woke up frisky today
    And had at her Grace,
    She kept doubling the pace
While the chambermaids shouted "Olé!"

78.

There was an old geezer named Blair,
Who used to get girls to strip bare
    By slipping red ants
    In their bras and their pants.
Yes, it works—but it lacks *savoir-faire*.

79.

In Vegas a hooker named Lou
Ran a number with one gent, then two.
    When a third asked to play
    She said, "Well, OK.
But that does it. *Rien ne vas plus*.

80.

Over beer in a dimly lit bar
I was puffing a ten-cent cigar,
    When a girl of a sort
    Said, "You look like a sport."
And my wife, in the shadows, said, "Ha!"

81.

Said Romeo climbing the fence,
"I love you, but this makes no sense.
    That damned wire has ripped
    My left ball and snipped
Both my prepuce and vas deferens."

82.

"Shall we?" said Fred pinching Flo,
"Or are you as pure as the snow?"
    "That's two questions," said she,
    "And my answer must be
—If you've got fifty bucks—yes and no."

83.

A writer has got to be deft.
When he finds he has no money left,
    Can he do without meals?
    To hell with ideals.
Learn to toss off a *roman à cleft*.

8 4 .

A raffiné poet named Potz
Took a rather high view of the otz.
    He was quick to proclaim
    His hard gemlike flame,
But the best he could manage was quotz.

8 5 .

There was a young husband named Dan,
Who set up his wife in a van
    And sent her to park
    Behind bars after dark.
It is hard to think well of that man.

8 6 .

Imprudent and unwed Mae-Bette
Had to shop for a basic layette.
    When they told her the price
    She gasped once or twice,
But she paid. And has more to pay yet.

8 7 .

A mechanic who married a shrew
Got her tamed in a minute or two.
    He just took out his kit
    And fiddled a bit.
All it took was a turn of the screw.

8 8 .

At the orgy last night Dionysus
In a rather remarkable nisus
    Had ten maids, a goat,
    Four pink boys, and a shoat
In sixteen consecutive trices.

8 9 .

There once was a wife who was sure
She was right. And she was. Till a whore
    Who was glad to be wrong
    Sang the old boy a song,
And they ran off to Cannes. *Vive l'amour!*

9 0 .

There was a young dumpling from Boulder
Who loved to ride dear daddy's shoulder.
    Dad, at first, thought it fun.
    Then she turned twenty-one,
And he thought she should know—so he told her.

9 1 .

There once was a cocky Eurasian
Who kept rising to every occasion.
    From what I have heard,
    When nothing occurred
He still rose, by sheer self-persuasion.

9 2 .

A learned and truly exquisite
Young miss paid her tutor a visit.
    When, testing her thesis,
    He suggested syncresis,
She responded, in form, "V*idilicet*."

9 3 ·

There was a young man from St. Kitt's
With an itch that was giving him fits.
    It seems that a peach
    He picked up on the beach
Had left his bed full of strange nits.

9 4 ·

On the ski slopes young Dr. MacPrutt
Hit an ice slick and lit on his butt
    On a jagged rock shelf
    Thus divesting himself
Of what laymen would call his left nut.

9 5 ·

A gracious young hostess named Ewing
Believed she had only been doing
    Her ladylike best
    To welcome a guest,
And was startled when he called it "screwing."

9 6 .

A meticulous young dean named Lester
Took a girl to his rooms and undressed her.
    Then took out some charts
    And compared all her parts
With the norms for the current semester.

9 7 .

There was an old miser of whom
Little good could be said. I presume
    His cash did him credit.
    But, though no one said it,
He stank like the dungheap of Doom.

9 8 .

A puny Greek stripling named Kimon
Turned into a sexual demon
    After praying to Hera
    For various sera
Compounded of powdered goat semen.

9 9 ·

I suppose it did seem indiscrete
Of Myra to dance down the street
    With her all on display.
    Yet, at bottom, I'd say
The impulse was really quite sweet.

1 0 0 .

A chap who was sailing for Singapore
Left room in his seabag to bring a whore
    Then forgot that he had
    Until she turned bad,
Which tended to make the whole thing a bore.

1 0 1 .

A proper young miss who got stewed
Awoke rather shockingly nude
    In a room with six gents
    And a terrified sense
That she had been—and was being—screwed.

1 0 2 .

There was a young man who give chase
To loose women—a pitiful case
    Made more sordid by wine,
    Till, at seventy-nine,
He died with an evil grimace.

1 0 3 .

South of Nome there's a farmer I know
Whose fields are all covered with snow
    From September to May
    When the stuff melts away
Leaving just time for nothing to grow.

1 0 4 .

At the last dance a scoundrel from Media
Picked a wallflower and whispered, "I needia!"
    Said the maiden undaunted,
    It's nice to be wanted,
But you could have been just a bit speedia."

1 0 5 .

In the north woods a girl from St. Jacques
Was willing to give it a crack.
But her boyfriend, young Fred,
Kept pushing ahead
And circling to sneak up in back.

1 0 6 .

Said a busy young Texan in Rome,
Who had bought up the Vatican dome,
"It's not just for the art,
Though I'd say that's right smart,
It's the challenge of getting it home."

1 0 7 .

There was a young lady from Ipswich
Who grew famous for making her hips twitch
While shedding her clothes
Which, as one might suppose,
Were held on by no more than a slip stitch.

1 o 8 .

I won't say the girls at St. Francis
Intend to encourage lewd glances,
    But can one believe
    They are merely naïve
When they come in the nude to school dances?

1 o 9 .

There was an old salt on the Banks
Who said to a mermaid, "No thanks.
    The last time I tried
    Those scales took my hide
Clear off from my crotch to my shanks."

1 1 o .

An elegant lady named Pruitt
Did not absolutely eschew it
    But demanded such bowing
    And scraping and vowing
That most gents walked out saying, "Screw it!"

1 1 1 .

Our German prof, Doktor von Strüss,
Is not one to play fast and loose,
But at faculty do's,
Having sampled the booze,
He's been known to try out a sly goose.

1 1 2 .

Said a Washington hostess named Moll
To a subclerk she passed in the hall,
"Once his Excellency goes,
I should like to propose
That we not stand on strict protocol."

1 1 3 .

At the Last Chance Saloon good old Mabel
Used to put all her cards on the table,
And herself on request.
If she wasn't the best,
She was open, aboveboard, and able.

1 1 4 .

Said a well-preserved harlot named Gwen,
"I have chalked up my three score and ten.
    I can't ask for much more,
    But I'm going for four,
And maybe I'll stop scoring then."

1 1 5 .

A well-heeled old dame named Roberta
Had been brought up to think sex would hurta.
    But she found, in the main,
    A high threshhold of pain
Was an asset that would not deserta.

1 1 6 .

There was a young lady from Butte
Who acted a little too cute,
    Especially for
    A five-dollar whore
In a house that lacked even repute.

1 1 7 .

There was a young man from Green Bay
Who awoke with a sense of dismay
    To find in his bed
    A girl who had read
All of Edna St. Vincent Millay.

1 1 8 .

At the Ritz a young lady drank lunch
With a roué who ordered rum punch.
    As they clinked cup to cup
    He said, "Well, bottom's up!"
—Which I'd say was a rather shrewd hunch.

1 1 9 .

There was a young lady from Deanstown
Who would have walked off with the queen's crown
    At the CYO rally
    Had not Father O'Malley
Caught her playing boy-girl with her jeans down.

1 2 0 .

There was an old hooker who blew.
What I mean is, she left town. If you
    Understood what I said
    To mean she gave head,
Well, I guess there was some of that, too.

1 2 1 .

Said a fair-skinned young lady named Nan
As she stretched on the beach, "I won't tan.
    Moonbeams are too thin
    To damage my skin
When I cover myself with a man."

1 2 2 .

Herr General von und zum Hallus
Had a caisson attached to his phallus,
    And would ride into battle
    With his brass balls a-rattle
While singing "Deutschland Über Alles!"

1 2 3 .

> At fair time Miz Flowerie-Belle Lee
> Takes in city gents for a fee.
>> But she lets us homefolk
>> Perch up in that oak
> By her winder and watch the show—free.

1 2 4 .

> Have you heard about poor Angelique?
> She canoed up the river last week
>> With some damn lumberjack.
>> And though they came back,
> We're afraid she's been left up the creek.

1 2 5 .

> There was a young lady named Lassiter,
> Whose permission could not have been taciter.
>> She would lie on the lawn
>> Barely stifling a yawn
> While our lads stood in line for a pass at her.

1 2 6 .

When he rode out the old laird of Clyde
Used to make it a matter of pride
  To scoop up a lass,
  Have a quick piece of ass,
And discard her without breaking stride.

1 2 7 .

There was a young lady named Jansen,
Whose Ma said, "I don't mind romancin'.
  You're young. Have your fling.
  But remember one thing:
When you stay out all night, keep on dancin'."

1 2 8 .

The first troops under Spanish command
To set foot on Floridian sand
  Found a Seminole maid
  Who took trinkets in trade
And gave them the lay of the land.

1 2 9 .

> An expert mechanic named Nims
> Kept a full range of foam-rubber shims
>   For adjusting the set
>   Of young ladies he'd get
> To indulge his meticulous whims.

1 3 0 .

> There was a young widow named Gormley,
> Who approached a young man quite inform'ly
>   And asked to be screwed.
>   "Please do not think me rude,"
> She explained, "I do not do this norm'ly."

1 3 1 .

> There once was an artist who drew
> Large crowds to blank canvases. "Ooh!"
>   Cried the critics, "the essence
>   Of the post-incandescence
> Of conceptualized déjà vu!"

1 3 2 .

An expensive young harlot named Ann
Just can't bear to say no to a man.
　　So for five bucks a week
　　She allows us a peek
On what she calls her lay-away plan.

1 3 3 .

There was a young person named Clarence,
Who cabled from Sweden: "Dear Parents:
　　Sex-change operation
　　Creates new relation.
As Clara, implore your forebearance."

1 3 4 .

There once was a girl from Piscataway
Who said to a school chum, "Is that a way
　　To treat an old friend?
　　You've got the wrong end.
Stop it, please. I do not like this thataway."

1 3 5 .

A middle-aged lady once reckoned
The passage of time to a second,
    Then rounded it out
    To ten years—just about—
Since the last man had come when she beckoned.

1 3 6 .

There once was a nervous young Finn
Who had barely begun to get in
    To a lady he knew
    When her husband said "Boo!"
—And he damned near jumped out of her skin.

1 3 7 .

There was a young man who drank rum.
In time he became a rank bum
    And his morals regressed.
    I have tried the same test
And I have to confess mine shrank some.

1 3 8 .

An impoverished young couple named Skeat
Used to bundle to save on the heat.
      But six kids in five years
      Left them in such arrears
They have never again made ends meet.

1 3 9 .

One day when a lady named Anne
Went up to the sun roof to tan
      A gent in a copter
      Flew over and dropped her
Some ads for a crash-diet plan.

1 4 0 .

Please take note of the ex Mrs. Tolliver.
Her husband tried making a doll of her.
      She did learn to blink,
      And say Papa, and wink.
But she found that did not express all of her.

1 4 1 .

At a gay bar two young men inspected
Some girls whom they promptly rejected
    In blank ennui.
    It was easy to see
They were totally other-directed.

1 4 2 .

There was a young lady named Kate,
Who found she was putting on weight.
    She requested a diet.
    Said her doctor, "Sure. Try it.
But your intake is more than you ate."

1 4 3 .

Here's a toast to my old sweetheart Sal,
A real down-home old-fashioned gal.
    For though once or twice
    She was busted for vice,
To me she was always a pal.

1 4 4 ·

What Asimov lacks of pure style
He makes up for—well, once in a while—
    By the way he can bluster
    From the depths of lackluster
To the (almost) transcendently vile.

The Authors

ISAAC ASIMOV emigrated from Russia when he was three years old. He received his B.S., M.A., and Ph.D. degrees from Columbia University. He is associate professor of chemistry at the Boston University School of Medicine and is the author of books on science for the general reader, science fiction, space, the solar system, mathematics, and other books of limericks and poems. His two hundredth book was recently published.

JOHN CIARDI, poet, educator, critic, has won countless awards, much praise, and a strong following for his own poetry. He was the poetry editor of the *Saturday Review* for sixteen years, director of the Bread Loaf Writers' Conference for seventeen years, and an essayist of both wit and powerful insight. His standard translation of *The Divine Comedy* is now available in a single-volume hardcover edition, for the first time complete and in final form.